Auth

This book features 100 influential and inspiring quotes by Michael Scott. Undoubtedly, this collection will give you a huge boost of inspiration.

1

"If I had a gun with two bullets and I was in a room with Hitler, Bin Laden, and Toby, I would shoot Toby twice."

2

"I saved a life. My own. Am I a her? I really can't say, but yes!"

3

"Would I rather be feared or loved? Easy. Both. I want people to be afraid of how much they love me."

4

"Wikipedia is the best thing ever. Anyone in the world can write anything they want about any subject. So you know you are getting the best possible information."

5

"Guess what, I have flaws. What are they? Oh, I don't know. I sing in the shower. Sometimes I spend too much time volunteering. Occasionally I'll hit somebody with my car. So sue me."

6

"No, I'm not going to tell them about the downsizing. If a patient has cancer, you don't tell them."

7

"An office is not for dying. An office is a place for living life to the fullest, to the max, to... an office is a place where dreams come true."

8

"Do I need to be liked? Absolutely not. I like to be liked. I enjoy being liked. I have to be liked, but it's not like this compulsive need to be liked, like my need to be praised.

9

"Sometimes I'll start a sentence, and I don't even know where it's going. I just hope I find it along the way."

10

"Do I have a special someone? Well, yeah, of course. A bunch of 'em. My employees.

11

"They say on your deathbed you never wish you spent more time at the office — but I will."

12

"Make friends first, make sales second, make love third. In no particular order."

13

"I love inside jokes. I hope to be
a part of one someday."

14

"I'm an early bird and a night owl. So I'm wise and have worms."

15

"Well, it's love at first sight. Actually, it was... no, it was when I heard her voice. It was love at first see with my ears."

16

"The most sacred thing I do is care and provide for my workers, my family. I give them money. I give them food. Not directly, but through the money."

17

"I wanna be married and have 100 kids so I can have 100 friends and no one can say 'no' to being my friend."

18

"I feel like all my kids grew up and then they married each other. It's every parent's dream."

19

"You know what they say 'Fool me once, strike one, but fool me twice... strike three.'"

20

"I know it's illegal in Pennsylvania, but it's for charity, and I consider myself a great philanderer."

21

"Two queens at casino night. I am gonna drop a deuce on everybody."

22

"I don't understand. We have a day honoring Martin Luther King, but he didn't even work here."

23

"I'm not superstitious but I am a little stitious."

24

"Now, you may look around and see two groups here. White-collar, blue-collar. But I don't see it that way. And you know why not? Because I am collar-blind."

25

"And I'm optimistic because every day I get a little more desperate."

26

"I am Beyonce, always."

27

"It's not like booze ever killed anyone."

28

"And I knew exactly what to do. But in a much more real sense, I had no idea what to do."

29

"The worst thing about prison
was the dementors."

30

"There's no such thing as an appropriate joke. That's why it's called a joke."

31

"Society teaches us that having feelings and crying is bad and wrong. Well, that's baloney, because grief isn't wrong. There's such a thing as good grief. Just ask Charlie Brown."

32

"I say dance, they say 'How high?'"

33

"Tell him to call me ASAP as possible."

34

"Presents are the best way to show how much you care. It's a tangible thing you can point at and say, 'Hey man, I love you. This many dollars worth.'"

35

"Dwight, you ignorant slut."

36

"I want you to rub butter on my foot... Pam, please? I have Country Crock."

37

"There is no greater feeling than when two people who are perfect for each other overcome all obstacles and find true love."

38

"I would say I kind of have an unfair advantage because I watch reality dating shows like a hawk, and I learn. I absorb information from the strategies of the winners and the losers. Actually, I probably learn more from the losers."

39

"About 40 times a year, Michael gets sick but has no symptoms. Dwight is always gravely concerned."

40

"There were these huge bins of clothes and everybody was rifling through them like crazy. And I grabbed one and it fit! So, I don't think that this is totally just a woman's suit. At the very least it's bisexual."

41

"Any man who says he totally understands women is a fool. Because they are un-understandable."

42

"When the son of the deposed king of Nigeria emails you directly, asking for help, you help! His father ran the freaking country! OK?"

43

"I had a great summer. I got West Nile virus, lost a ton of weight. Then I went back to the lake. And I stepped on a piece of glass in the parking lot, which hurt. That got infected. Even though I peed on it."

44

"Friends joke with one another. 'Hey, you're poor.' 'Hey, your mama's dead.' That's what friends do."

45

"I am running away from my responsibilities. And it feels good."

46

"Toby is in HR, which technically means he works for corporate. So he's not really a part of our family. Also, he's divorced, so he's not really a part of his family."

47

"Saw Inception. Or at least I
dreamt I did."

48

"Jan is cold. If she was sitting across from you on a train and she wasn't moving, you might think she was dead."

49

"Number eight. Learn how to take off a woman's bra: You just twist your hand until something breaks.

50

"I don't come up with this stuff, I just forward it along. You wouldn't arrest the guy who was just passing drugs from one guy to another."

51

"I love my employees even though I hit one of you with my car."

52

"I would not miss it for the world. But if something else came up, I would definitely not go."

53

"This is our receptionist, Pam. If you think she's cute now, you should have seen her a couple years ago."

54

"Like right here is my favorite New York pizza joint. And I'm going to go get me a New York slice."

55

"Sometimes you have to take a break from being the kind of boss that's always trying to teach people things. Sometimes you just have to be the boss of dancing."

56

"I would say I kind of have an unfair advantage because I watch reality dating shows like a hawk, and I learn. I absorb information from the strategies of the winners and the losers. Actually, I probably learn more from the losers."

57

"Nobody likes beets, Dwight! Why don't you grow something that everybody does like? You should grow candy."

58

"It takes you thirty seconds to brush your teeth? Wow, that's ten times as long as it takes me."

59

"I took her to the hospital. And the doctors tried to save her life, they did the best they could. And she is going to be OK."

60

"Yes, it is true. I, Michael Scott, am signing up with an online dating service. Thousands of people have done it, and I am going to do it. I need a username. And I have a great one. Little Kid Lover. That way people will know exactly where my priorities are at."

61

"People will never be replaced by machines. In the end, life and business are about human connections. And computers are about trying to murder you in a lake. And to me the choice is easy."

62

"Hi, I'm Date Mike. Nice to meet me. How do you like your eggs in the morning?"

63

"I've got to make sure that YouTube comes down to tape this."

64

"OK, too many different words from coming at me from too many different sentences."

65

"The people that you work with are, when you get down to it, your very best friends."

66

"Webster's Dictionary defines wedding as 'the fusing of two metals with a hot torch.'"

67

"Granted, maybe this was not the best idea, but at least we care enough about our employees that we are willing to fight for them."

68

"I guess the attitude that I've tried to create here is that I'm a friend first and a boss second and probably an entertainer third."

69

"Reverse psychology is an awesome tool. I don't know if you guys know about it, but, basically, you make someone think the opposite of what you believe. And that tricks them into doing something stupid. Works like a charm."

70

"I am Michael, and I am part English, Irish, German, and Scottish... sort of a virtual United Nations."

71

"If you don't like it, Stanley, you can go to the back of the bus, or the front of the bus, or drive the bus."

72

"If you break that girl's heart, I will kill you. That's just a figure of speech. But seriously, if you break that girl's heart, I will literally kill you and your entire family."

73

"My mind is going a mile an hour."

74

"It's a pimple, Phyllis. Avril Lavigne gets them all the time, and she rocks harder than anyone alive."

75

"Is there something besides 'Mexican' you prefer to be called? Something less offensive?"

76

"It just seems awfully mean. But sometimes, the ends justify the mean."

77

"No, Rose, they are not breathing. And they have no arms or legs... Where are they? You know what? If we come across somebody with no arms or legs, do we bother resuscitating them? I mean, what quality of life do we have there?"

78

"Abraham Lincoln once said that, 'If you're a racist, I will attack you with the North.' And those are the principles that I carry with me in the workplace."

79

"They say that your wedding day goes by in such a flash that you're lucky if you even get a piece of your own cake. I say that's crazy. I say let them eat cake. Margaret Thatcher said that about marriage. Smart broad."

80

"Here it is, heart of New York City, Times Square... named for the good times you have when you're in it."

81

"Two weeks ago, I was in the worst relationship of my life. She treated me poorly, we didn't connect, I was miserable. Now, I am in the best relationship of my life, with the same woman. Love is a mystery."

82

"You will not die! Stanley! Stanley! Barack is President! You are black, Stanley!"

83

"I want today to be a beautiful memory that the staff and I share after I have passed on to New York. And if Toby is a part of it, then it'll suck."

84

"I think Angela might be gay. Could Oscar and Angela be having a gay affair? Maybe! Is that what this is about?"

85

"That was offensive and lame. So double offensive. This is an environment of welcoming and you should just get the hell out of here."

86

"Oh, this is gonna feel so good getting this thing off my chest... that's what she said."

87

"Well, well, well, how the turntables."

88

"We're all homos. Homo...
Sapiens."

89

"You cheated on me? When I specifically asked you not to?"

90

"I don't want any special treatment, Pam. I just want you to treat me like you would some family member who's undergone some sort of serious physical trauma. I don't think that's too much to ask?"

91

"I enjoy having breakfast in bed. I like waking up to the smell of bacon, sue me. And since I don't have a butler, I do it myself. So, most nights before I go to bed, I will lay six strips of bacon out on my George Foreman Grill. Then I go to sleep. When I wake up, I plug in the grill, I go back to sleep again. Then I wake up to the smell of crackling bacon."

92

"Hate to see you leave, but love to watch you go. 'Cause of your butt."

93

"Well, happy birthday, Jesus. Sorry that your party's so lame."

94

"It's a good thing Russia doesn't exist anymore."

95

"I hate so much about the things you choose to be."

96

"That's what she said!"

"Occasionally, I'll hit someone with my car. So sue me."

98

"I learned a while back that if I do not text 911, people do not return my calls. Um, but now people always return my calls because they think that something horrible has happened."

99

"I live by one rule: No office romances, no way. Very messy, inappropriate... no. But, I live by another rule: Just do it... Nike."

100

"The rules of shotgun are very simple and very clear. The first person to shout 'shotgun' when you're within sight of the car gets the front seat. That's how the game's played. There are no exceptions for someone with a concussion."

Made in the USA
Las Vegas, NV
06 December 2022

61010455R00056